My Eightieth

BRIAN COX retired as John Ed
Literature at Manchester Un
guished career. In 1959 he fou
Quarterly with A.E. Dyson. He became famous in 1969 as one
of the editors of the highly controversial Black Papers on
Education, and again in 1989 when he chaired the government
committee which set up the National Curriculum in English.
His book about the curriculum, *Cox on Cox*, became a best-
seller. After his retirement he became Chair of North West Arts,
which involved two years as a member of the Arts Council, and
Chair of the Arvon Foundation. He has lectured for the British
Council in France, Brazil, India, Hong Kong, Australia and
South Korea. Brian Cox has published many books of literary
criticism, an autobiography and four books of poetry.

Also by Brian Cox from Carcanet Press

Collected Poems
Emeritus

BRIAN COX

My Eightieth Year to Heaven

For Andrew, with much
admiration for your new
book of poems.

Brian Summer, 2007

CARCANET

Acknowledgements

Some of these poems have previously appeared in *Critical Quarterly*, *PN Review* and *The Sewanee Review*.

Lines from 'Poem in October' by Dylan Thomas from *The Collected Poems* (Dent) reproduced by permission of David Higham Associates. In the United States, from *The Poems of Dylan Thomas*, copyright © 1945 by The Trustees for the Copyrights of Dylan Thomas, first published in *Poetry*. Reprinted by permission of New Directions Publishing Corp.

First published in Great Britain in 2007 by
Carcanet Press Limited
Alliance House
Cross Street
Manchester M2 7AQ

A CIP catalogue record for this book is available from the British Library
ISBN 978 1 85754 931 7

The publisher acknowledges financial assistance from Arts Council England

Typeset by XL Publishing Services, Tiverton
Printed and bound in England by SRP Ltd, Exeter

for Jean and our family

It was my thirtieth
Year to heaven stood there then in the summer noon
Though the town below lay leaved with October blood.
O may my heart's truth
Still be sung
On this high hill in a year's turning.

Dylan Thomas, 'Poem in October'

Contents

Introduction   9

Shakespeare's Dream   13
Fox   14
Aboard the *Anacoluthe*   15
Moselle to the Rhine   17
La Villa Romaine Hotel, Carsac   18
Talmont on the Gironde   20
Canoe for Two   21
Canoe Again   23
Châtel-Guyon   24
Okefenokee   25
St Paul's Bay, Malta   27
Ephesus   28
Hermit   29
Doves   31
Jester   32
Ullswater Pastoral   33
Goblet   34
Cantaloupe   35
Old People Waking   36
Borges and Wordsworth   37
Darwin's *The Formation of Vegetable Mould Through
   the Action of Worms* (1881)   38
English Fowler   39
The Path to Rome   40
Louis de Bernières: *Birds Without Wings*   42
Great Expectations   44
Dickens's Fool and Saint   45
Tolstoy's Levin   46
Tolstoy's Oak   47
Seth's *Two Lives*   48
Pride and Prejudice: The Film   49
Privacy   50

Hospital   51
Prostate   52
Cheshire Walks   53
Reservoir   54
The Edge   55
Lake District   56
Flushes   57
Manchester United   58
Old Trafford   59
Sensation   60
Photographs   61
Jane Eyre in Derbyshire   62
End Game   63
Orhan Pamuk: *My Name is Red*   64

Introduction

Many of these poems grew out of personal experiences, some very personal: a short visit to a brand-new hotel in the Dordogne, reading Louis de Bernières' *Birds Without Wings* while suffering from a heavy cold, waiting in hospital for news about my prostate cancer. To some extent they make up a diary of some days which were interesting or important to me during the last seven or eight years. Therefore perhaps it's useful to start with a brief account of what happened to me in this time.

Lots of people find their sixties very enjoyable, particularly after retirement, but when we reach seventy many of us face difficult medical problems. This has certainly been my experience. After I retired in 1993 at the age of sixty-five as Professor of English Literature at the University of Manchester I continued to be busy. For six years I was Chair of North West Arts, which involved two years as a member of the Arts Council. I chaired the Arvon Foundation for three years. I also enjoyed acting as Poetry Editor for *Critical Quarterly* and, less enjoyably, I handled all the accounts. My wife and I had free time for extensive holidays in France, Germany, Cyprus, Crete, New York and South Africa. We were typical healthy pensioners. In 2001, when I was seventy-three, I discovered I had prostate cancer.

My work for North West Arts meant I was involved in decisions far more influential than any in my previous career, even when I was Pro-Vice-Chancellor at Manchester University. I argued strongly and successfully on the Arts Council for lottery funding for the wonderful Lowry Centre at Salford, a project opposed by art critics such as Brian Sewell and London members of the Arts Council. I was heavily involved in solving the financial problems of the Royal Exchange Theatre in Manchester after the IRA bomb made it possible the theatre might never reopen. The poems in my last collection of verse, *Emeritus* (Carcanet, 2001) were almost all written during this period. Since I retired as Chair of North West Arts in 2000 I've spent more time in writing verse. The poems in this new collection were all written in these recent years. I love the business of composition, the false starts, the crossings out, the arduous search for the right word. I often quote Auden's advice: if your son holds high ideals make him a preacher; if he loves playing with words make him a poet.

During the years I've been writing these new poems the world has witnessed terrifying events: the destruction of the Twin Towers in New York, the massacre of children at Beslan and the war in Iraq. I was once asked at a poetry reading why I dealt with what might seem relatively unimportant issues. My answer was in two parts. First, I've nothing to say about these tragic events which is in any way original. I'm unable to find words for my feelings of shock and impotence. Second, I believe it's important to record unique, individual moments. Celebration of the variety of human life is an admirable aim for all writers. I called my first book of poems *Every Common Sight* (London Magazine Editions, 1981), a quotation from Wordsworth. Like him, I feel even the most ordinary experiences can be filled with wonder. I've no faith in large-scale political solutions. Like Karl Popper, I'm unsympathetic to blueprints for total change, to 'holistic' solutions, and think we must try to solve immediate small problems rather than set out on some utopian revolutionary path to change the world.

When in 2001 my prostate cancer was diagnosed, the condition was so far advanced, with some spread into the bones, that an operation to remove the prostate would have been a waste of time. The treatment involved pills and Zoladex injections, which reduce testosterone, on which the cancer feeds. I suffered some months of discomfort before my body began to cope better with this treatment, and I returned to normal living. The hospital told me that when this treatment works patients usually survive about five years, sometimes more. My doctor called the cancer 'lethargic', a word I've learnt to treasure. By the summer of 2002 I was back to playing tennis again (badly) and to my favourite walks in Cheshire and Derbyshire. Ted Hughes once told me the major problem for a poet was to find a new idea for a poem, and although technical difficulties with language might take time, once he had an idea he knew he would finish the poem. At least my prostate cancer gave me a few ideas for poems. Since my condition was first diagnosed, I've enjoyed several years of great happiness. I hope the poems about prostate cancer in this collection will encourage fellow sufferers.

Brian Cox, 2007

Shakespeare's Dream

for Jean, in our Golden Wedding Year, 2004

They're amateurs, but still when Puck
orates his final rhymes, takes stock
of all that we have seen, he speaks
so well the ancient magic works
once more, and I'm entranced by words
I've known and loved for sixty years.

Yet since at school I played my part
as Theseus, moonshine has lost
its lustre, and I concur with Pepys
who thought the play ridiculous,
and I concur with Theseus
who thought young lovers lunatics.

But Shakespeare's poetry remains
beyond the art of modern words.
Its music plays from distant shores,
from ideal worlds where wild thyme blows,
where city wits in magic woods
confess the might of other gods.

Puck calls the play an idle show,
but we schoolchildren long ago
never forgot this hymn to joy,
to married love, so in our play
Theseus relished word and rhyme.
He married Cobweb in due time.

Fox

Sleepless I slip from bed to contemplate
a shadow taking form, and all at once

our anti-burglar lights illuminate.
An urban fox lopes past my garden shed,

and then, slowly, with splendid impudence
ambles across my special flower bed

to stop and stare at me as if he owned
my bright-lit lawn, and dared me to dispute

his right to stay down there, enthroned
like one of Hughes's mystic animals.

Ted's fox – its sharp, hot stink – quickened his thought,
fertilised art like pagan rituals,

while I distrust his cult of violence,
for animals may never understand

the civil arts – kindness and tolerance,
good will on which the best of days depend.

My urban fox at last decides to scoot.
He bears no wisdom I can ever want –

bold scavenger, just that, of eggs and fruit.

Aboard the *Anacoluthe*

Saga holidays are restricted to people over the age of fifty

Our guide translates its name as 'oxymoron';
this barge hotel does not forget its past.
Its dirty petrol transport days contrast
with four-star comfort cruising down the Seine.

And we are living oxymorons too.
Southwards, tasting our wine, *premier cru*,
youthful in age, we Saga tourists flow
from Paris slowly on to Fontainebleau.

I've not been here before, but many times
I've read in Maupassant or Henry James
of sunlit lovers rowing down the Seine,
of landscapes rosy-tinted by champagne,

of Henriette in Maupassant's short tale
who with her handsome oarsman must obey
when he in secret island hideaway
makes her sit still to hear a nightingale,

and, while she must not move, circles her waist,
and I with him, aged sixteen, reading this,
yearn for new happiness, at last to taste
a girl's complete submission to my kiss.

In James, Strether seeks rest in rural France,
abandons duty, drifts by happenstance –
as I've so often done in winter dream –
to dine outdoors beside a grey-blue stream

and watch two lovers in a skiff float round
the bend, Madame de Vionnet and Chad,
so intimate, at ease, the climax where
Strether perceives the truth of Chad's affair.

So while today under a pearl-grey sky
old couples watch green landscapes slipping by,
we bear with us rich images of youth,
dream-like mixtures of falsity and truth;

and as our barge negotiates the locks
past Henrietta's hideaway, Strether's inn,
what I've read mingles with what I've done:
I've lived here all my life, among these books.

Moselle to the Rhine

Our Rhine Princess descends through locks
from Cochem slowly moving down
until we float in noon-day light
beside a little Moselle town:
half-timbered houses, clean and white,
steep vineyards reaching up the hills,
a fairy-tale, so peaceful, yet

dark castles from a picture-book
fought wars we easily forget.
We pass Koblenz, then journey south
to moor all day at Rüdesheim.
A band disrupts the village square,
watchers clap, and dance in line,
drums are banged and trumpets blare;

and yet just sixty years ago
our friends dropped bombs along the Rhine
where we today with German youth
sit in a bar and drink our wine.
Next day we journey back to Köln.
Our cabin TV shows Iraq
where bombs still fall and children die.

Steep gangways lead us to the deck,
crowded, as we identify
the famous bridge at Remegen.
We're lucky to survive. Wars never cease.
As round the river bend we see
distant cathedral spires at Köln
old people share a fragile peace.

La Villa Romaine Hotel, Carsac

In Latin 'private' means 'deprived',
unfit for public livelihood.

Villa Romaine, Dordogne habitat,
opened last week, a Greco-Roman site

behind an ornamental gate
workmen still sweat to keep erect.

Driven by heat, we take a room
climatisée, and we're alone,

the only guests, as from the road
late vans discharge their final load.

We rest upon a king-size bed
behind silk curtains like a shroud

that gently sways and undulates:
coolness in air-conditioned bliss.

This summer heat creates a scene
as if inside a picture frame:

a river where no water runs,
flowers in Japanese gardens

– lotus, orchids – so fixed and still
it's like a living aquarelle.

The kitchen isn't ready yet
and so we try a 'set repast':

melon, salmon, local wines,
one waiter-cook to serve our needs.

And yet next day the glamour fades.
We're special here, like kings and queens

compelled to live in palaces,
always subject to servants' eyes.

A gardener leaning on his spade
watches our swim, and then a maid

post-lunch when we've read and snoozed
insists on making up our bed.

Small things indeed, a pleasant pause,
but now we wish to be ourselves,

to take the road towards Bordeaux,
leaving behind this public show,

driving across the Carsac bridge,
and no one knows the way we go:

'private' today means 'privilege'.

Talmont on the Gironde

for A.E. Dyson, 1928–2002

At Talmont pilgrims paused and prayed
en route for Compostella: paused
to worship miracles, while we
stop here to marvel that the sea
never destroyed this little church,
perilous on its rocky perch.

An ancient graveyard overrun
by flowers, bright in midday sun
– ground lilac, roses, hollyhock –
welcomes us and makes me think
of Tony, friend of fifty years,
who would have loved these quiet ways.

Inside the church, stone-cool and calm,
two euros buy a candle flame.
I've not observed these rites before.
I light the wick, and then withdraw
to gaze at flowers beyond the porch.
I feel you're here: our final watch.

Canoe for Two

Our mini-bus bounces twelve miles
by rues deformées, tree-lined lanes
that lead upstream to portage where
unwise adventurers prepare

in small canoes to brave the Tarn.
Our host, his only thought to earn
his rental fee, provides no guide,
launches us down the chute beside

the weir, and then drives back, while we,
sopping wet, paddle jerkily
downstream between high canyon crags,
making progress in long zigzags

as we improve our water skill,
relishing noon-day sun until
white water gleams around a curve.
At first it's not so hard to swerve

past hidden stones and plummet down
towards a pool, a safer zone
where we may swim and eat our food.
But soon ahead two rocks protrude

and it's too late for us to turn.
We slew sideways, both bow and stern
held firm. As water starts to ship
across the side, I roll and flop

into the spate; the lightened craft
bobs jauntily, and with a swift
descent drags me, clinging on,
to scrape my way across each stone.

Crowds picnic in a sunlit field
to watch and laugh, sometimes applaud,
as each canoe attempts to dodge
black rocks that line a fearsome gorge.

This time we win, and navigate
with such aplomb each narrow strait
the cynic watchers on the shore
salute us with a modest cheer.

Canoe Again

All that so many years ago:
and now in age we choose to flow
in smoother streams, to float eight miles,
paddling with ease Dordogne ways

where no white water interferes,
no chutes beside alarming weirs,
riding sedately by long lines
of poplar trees and castle walls.

We stop for lunch, and I feel sad
we can't make present time recede.
I'd take that mini-bus again,
canoe white waters down the Tarn.

I sip my Kir. That's just a dream.
We'll keep on paddling with the stream.

Châtel-Guyon

Across the valley floor
florid hotels gaze out
forlornly in the growing dusk,
like Buxton,
grand showy façades,
masks hiding empty corridors
where once Parisian élites
smirked and flounced.

The ancient spa lays on
live concerts in the park.
A Cuban group brings back to life
a bandstand floodlit in the gloom:
waltz, beguine, mazurka.
An old man beats two sticks
setting the music's time,
while Gerard Tarquin, maestro,
struts about the stage
blowing his clarinet as if
he'd make the flowers jump up
and dance along their silent beds.

It's cold. The listeners drift away:
behind them Tarquin never stops,
aiming his clarinet
towards the empty seats.

Okefenokee

Flat-bottomed boats push slowly through the swamps
by cypress trees festooned with Spanish moss.
Black alligators watch us as we pass.

We're told we're safe, that alligators don't
eat men, just dogs, that golfers feel no threat
putting a ball beside a long-nosed snout.

Back at the lodge a Lawrence gipsy type,
basket in hand, is paid to show our group
a rattlesnake he woke up from its nap

that very dawn. He's here to demonstrate
these snakes won't move, however much provoked,
towards a man. The small room empties fast.

But some of us remain, as he condemns
the falsities of Hollywood, and then unloads
onto the floor six feet of writhing coils.

The snake curls up beside the wall, and waits;
he claims its terrified, and when he pokes
at it with two-pronged, wooden fork, it strikes

back at the teasing wood, rattles its tail,
but never leaves its station by the wall.
We even feel a bond with its ordeal.

I've parked my Rambler car beside the spot
where just one month ago a woman left
her poodle near her car in midday heat

safe on its lead, except no one had told
the alligators not to break the code.
When she returned she found only the lead.

I drive away across the border dyke.
The lodge looks flimsy in the growing dark.

St Paul's Bay, Malta

Small fishing boats, bright greens and blues,
sport on their prow black slitted eyes

of Osiris to ward off jinns;
and yet they give their craft the names

of saints. They're faithful Christian souls
who won't defy the pagan gods.

St Paul was shipwrecked on these shores.
This is a site for miracles:

he strikes a rock and water flows,
he hurls a viper in the flames.

Our local bus is forced to stop
beside a crowded square. We gawp

at Paul in effigy, serene,
as white-smocked youths await the sign

to lift their load on poles and start
his ride to bless each ancient street.

He's eight feet tall, in blue and white.
Old ways stay undefeated yet.

Ephesus

on the day the Archbishop of Canterbury hosted a conference
in London on homosexuality, 2003

Our group includes two Yorkshire gays;
they perch on stones at Ephesus,
remains of fountains, arches, baths,
white broken colonnades where once
Apostle Paul spoke famous words
that reach across the centuries,

so children still today are told
that love is patient, love is kind.
Yet prophecies have failed, the end
he dreamt did not materialise,
and all that scorn for sex and gays
has poisoned lives, still poisons lives.

We end our day with apple tea.
Our Yorkshire friends praise Roman arts
– great Artemis with flowing breasts –
and say the best of Paul still lives,
his faith and hope and charity,
while bishops stoop to throw their stones.

Hermit

We walk uphill through sloping fields
to Saint Avit, whose abbey points
its towers towards a cloudless sky.

Avicus chose to live and die
in cold, a damp and grubby cave
among wild beasts, perched on a hill

where he performed his daily drill
of prayer, healing the sick with powers
the village knew dropped straight from God.

Stones rose to keep off rain and wind.
The church they built grew like a strange
and gorgeous tree, in whose calm shade

the pilgrims found their lives remade
by faith in miracles, in shrines,
relics whose touch would cure their pain.

Such faith we never can regain.
The pilgrims seem another race
whose ways of thought we can't repeat,

and yet not everything is lost;
we stop inside the church to find
we're all alone, in silence that

demands we act with due respect:
an inkling of the numinous
beneath high arches in the nave.

Saint Avicus, inside his cave,
knew just such hints of paradise.
Outside, as we descend the slope,

the sunlit fields seem touched with hope.

Doves

Two pure white doves settled beneath our eaves,
and I was glad to welcome them,
to hear at dawn their murmurings
bestowing on my day a gentle benison.

Under the overhang they built a nest,
snug, dry, where as the weeks passed by
they looked so self-possessed,
staring unmoved while I gazed back at them.

By June we'd gained a second family;
from the nest's shadow a white speck
turned into two young doves, looking at me
as I unlocked the car, set off for work.

But all this time their droppings made a mess;
our gutters clogged with gunge
which neighbours said was poisonous.
Our sloping roof was leaking like a sponge.

we hired a local handyman named Mike,
whose water jets blasted the tiles,
who built a mesh of wickerwork to block
their access to their nest beneath the eaves.

For days and weeks the doves patrolled
the roof. Today all four are watching me.
They're keeping very still. They look appalled.

Jester

In dreams last night
I biked away from home
pursued by half-glimpsed
gunmen in the gloom.
At traffic lights
I felt I had to stop
and leant exhausted
up against the lamp,
while menace closed the gap.

The post wobbled, then cracked;
it leant skew-whiff,
lights winking on and off
while buses honked reproof.
Expert pole-vaulter,
I clung on tight,
sailing over the bar,
holding my bike
happy at last as I awoke.

So who or what makes up
these lurid, zany tales?
Freud doesn't help
by simplifying dreams;
in sleep the day's events
tumble in disarray
coerced by madcap wit:
this strange creative force,
this jester in the night.

Ullswater Pastoral

'The Church Hotel from Sharrow Bay';
my watercolour landscape peers
at me, asking what attitudes
permit a moment's holiday

from nightmares in the daily news.
This is the art of yesteryear.
The Church Hotel's white walls appear
like dots against encircling fells,

but stillness on this placid lake
poses no threat. Within their frame
blue hills reflect old-fashioned calm
when every moment stands unique.

The frames that held this art in place
are shattered now, and chaos lives;
yet order still can speak to us,
offer perhaps a touch of grace.

Goblet

On New Year's Day we take our child
to watch the bathers brave the cold.
An ancient lighthouse, now restored,

reveals Whitehaven history;
through storms across the Irish sea
tobacco, sugar, rum, and slaves;

the Beilby glass, exquisite craft,
engraved with royal arms to fête
the launch of slaver *Royal George*.

Our boy discovers weather games,
where he can pose on TV screens,
while I look out at harbour walls.

I call to him to see red lights:
ambulance, fire-engine, perhaps
to help a swimmer in distress.

Later we learn that while we played
and watched the ramblers on the road,
the cliff collapsed: one died;

we live our happiness through luck,
so fragile, like that Beilby glass.

Cantaloupe

for Pam Dellar, actress, died March, 2001

She sleeps downstairs. Parked in our hall
her cylinder of air with all

its weird accoutrements breathes through
long nights, her emphysema due

to ignorance, to brio days
smoking her way through post-war plays,

mouthing her lines when etiquette
entailed that tribal cigarette.

At Cheadle Hulme when trains run late
and girls stand smoking while we wait,

she talks to them, showing the hose
connecting oxygen to nose.

Back home I play my old CDs,
among them ancient Auvergne songs

she's never heard before: across the hills
the simple love-lorn shepherd fills

hot summer days with sounds so rare
she finds their beauty hard to bear.

The service at her funeral
includes the Auvergne pastoral;

as we depart we're leaving here
a life whose loss it's hard to bear.

Old People Waking

Geese honk across the park
announcing winter dawn,

while gentle nasal clicks
betray you're still asleep.

Across the bed I hear
the central heating creak

and in the morning street
smooth cars set off for work.

Retired, I'm free at last.
I wait for you to stir.

Borges and Wordsworth

Blind men enjoy the touch of morning winds
in ways beyond the ken of sighted friends.
Borges did not resent his tragedy

but used his plight to serve his art, happy
to savour his growing blindness, like one
who contemplates a slowly setting sun.

It's February and I'm raking leaves.
Across my lawn the sun casts light green lines
so I can see where moss displaces grass.

I'm overwhelmed by all this loveliness.
Wordsworth was wrong. I find that now I'm old
I greet each extra day like some new friend:

sharpness of sense no youth may understand.

Darwin's *The Formation of Vegetable Mould Through the Action of Worms* (1881)

Darwin enjoyed the company of worms.
On summer nights he crept lightfoot downstairs
to check their secret ways, to stand amazed
while underneath his feet slow buttings turned
the garden soil. Even the heaviest of stones
sank down beneath the moonlit tasks of worms.

To test their sense he tried a dozen tricks,
maintaining them indoors in pots for weeks
while Francis played bassoon and Emma banged
piano keys to test if they detected sound.
He blew shrill whistles, breathed tobacco fumes,
waved red hot pokers, measuring their moves.

At Stonehenge Darwin grubbed around the base
of fallen stones, recording every trace
of worm activity, but better still
at Abinger he watched men humping soil
to clear a Roman pavement where he could
record the worm tilth marks for each decade.

So why should we spend time in scrutinising words
about an old man scrutinising worms?
Symbols lie lurking here, the simplest facts
upsetting old beliefs and ancient stones;
yet most of all we want to know the fads
and whims and quirks that make us men, not apes.

English Fowler

A nineteenth-century English gentleman:
at Rugby School he studied Greek, Latin,
taking for granted wisdom lurks in books.
In sick-bay once as fitting medicine
his master read him chunks of Browning's verse.

At Sedbergh School he taught for sixteen years
– Dura Virum Nutrix – stern nurse of men
and here he learnt the grandeur of the fells,
at dawn running to bathe in ice-cold streams,
taming Nature by classical routines.

In Guernsey he began his writing life,
at first translations, then he undertook
to lay down laws for English usage,
profound matters that led to bitter strife,
the use of colons, split infinitives.

Yet by attention to meaning's small shades
he helped to make English a living force,
a language, as we know, of rich brocades,
but capable of minute distinctions
vital for laws, for arts and sciences.

The Path to Rome

Hilaire Belloc vowed to hike from Toul
in northern France, alongside the Moselle,
through Alpine walls of ice, then to Milan,
over hot plains of Tuscany to Rome.

On this long pilgrimage he made three vows:
whenever possible to walk on straight
towards the South; never to ride on wheels,
to sleep rough, often journeying by night.

He dreamt of hours awake beneath the moon
after a meal of bread and ham and wine,
of heather banks looking up through the leaves
at all the summer splendour of the stars.

Instead he found himself cold, very cold,
above a bank of fog at Flavigny,
the moon dim, the fields dank, where he
soon learnt the joy of sleeping in a bed.

He planned to cross the Alps above the Rhône
over Gries Pass, avoiding tourist roads.
He hired a local guide, arose at three a.m.,
so determined to brave the darkening clouds

they both were soon in danger of their lives.
In storms of snow his guide made him turn back.
Defeated, he broke vows, compelled to make
a long detour by easy well-made roads.

And then his final problem. Two Bellocs
argued the way from Como to Milan:
to keep his vows, plod twenty-six
hot miles, or buy a ticket for the train.

I'm glad my Belloc chose the rolling wheels.
I like the man who learnt to compromise,
forgot his dreams, slept the last fifteen miles.

Louis de Bernières: *Birds Without Wings*

Caught by a winter cold I spend
five days inside a stranger's mind.
Warm winds across a Turkish plain
replace December rains, and I'm
so charmed by Persian sights and sounds
my coughing fits cannot erase
absorption in these ancient ways:
rags for the gods tied on red pines,
a potter at his daily task,
above the sea a golden mosque.

The potter tells of love and grief.
I'm hypnotised by village life,
communities of Greek and Turk
at peace without the need to mock
their rival faiths. In shades of pink
their simple houses carved from rock
stack up the valley slope, their folk
obedient to church or mosque,
while children roam the hills barefoot,
mixing at play without restraint.

The potter fashions local birds,
small terracotta figurines,
whose hollow tails he shapes to form
whistles, a present for his son
and friend who imitate the birds,
who fill the valleys with their calls.
Under his wicker canopy for shade
the potter claims he's like a god;
clothes caked in clay, he brings to birth
new things from water, fire and earth.

The boys grow up, depart for war.
Reading for me becomes a bore,
the battles of Gallipoli
reduced to turgid history.
Fiction more real than fact, I turn
the pages back again, rejoin
the potter and the village rites
where strangers rest like honoured guests,
where I'm at home inside old tales
of boys who copy nightingales.

Great Expectations

My angels may be blacksmiths.
I revere Joe Gargery,
a mild man forced to bear

with Pip his wife's rampages.
He couldn't read,
except for 'Js' and 'Os';

draped in penitential suit
with Pip in church he held
his prayer book upside down.

With clumsy boots, his hat
which toppled on the floor,
his country dialect,

he seemed a clown,
but kindness shaped his dignity.
Figure of fun, maybe, but yet

my perfect gentleman.

Dickens's Fool and Saint

Captain Cuttle tenders his friends
useless gifts, one old silver watch,
'two withered atomies of spoons',
'a pair of knock-kneed sugar tongs'.

Two bushy black eyebrows enrich
his weather-beaten countenance.
A hook instead of hand on wrist,
a broad blue suit and hard-glazed hat

seem fixed, like feathers on a bird.
Unfazed by those who think him mad,
he bends his mind to help his friends,
deep-seated, unfathomable schemes

which may not work out as he hopes,
but Florence, Walter, know he'd hop
from Charing Cross to Aldershot
if crazy plans might serve their needs.

When they sail back to London docks
he laughs along a busy street,
throwing his hard-glazed hat up high,
astounding all the passers-by.

Tolstoy's Levin

for Jean

When times are sad I like to muse
on Levin's happiness: the day
he watched his peasants mowing hay
and wondered whether he might choose

the simple life. Content to rest outdoors,
he spent the night under the stars
hearing the sound of marshland frogs,
distant barking of village dogs.

At dawn he walked the grassy roads
under a shell of fleecy clouds
until he heard her carriage wheels,
shaft-horses' hooves, tinkle of bells,

and then a glimpse of Kitty's face,
her honest eyes, her youthful grace,
so all at once his last night's schemes
were blown to shreds like empty dreams

Tolstoy's Oak

A great oak stands beside the road
in early spring, but doesn't yield

to green-shoot charms, gnarled hands so stern
its blackened bark reflects the scorn

Prince Andrew feels for those who trust
new spring brings happiness at last.

At Austerlitz the Prince lost hope,
content on his estates to help

the old and poor, until in May
Natasha's voice turns all that grey

to moonlit fantasy. When he
rides home, the oak beneath its canopy

of sappy, dark-green leaves berates
his apathy, his lifelessness.

Outside my window ancient oaks
in line beside our border dyke

recall these scenes; their grotesque shapes
deride the early daffodils,

and yet we know their bark still lives.
My wife takes out a tray of crumbs

and soon our garden fills with wings.
I'll live to prize the coming spring.

Seth's *Two Lives*

I'm reading Vikram Seth.
He tells of Auschwitz, where
his great-aunt's mother died:
her sister, Lola, too.

In archives at Jerusalem
on microfilm he finds
a list of those conveyed
in cattle trucks: Lola's name.

Cold bureaucratic words
detail their confiscated goods.
For weeks he cannot bear
to hear the German tongue.

Near Belsen once a friend
invited me to view the site.
I would not go. It felt
so wrong to tread the tourist path.

I love the feel of English words,
sweetness of rhyme and verse,
but my words never can express
such magnitude of grief.

Pride and Prejudice: **The Film**

Lyme Park's Palladian façade
looks down on me beside the pond
where Darcy in white shirt once plunged,

except if he leapt here he'd land
in shallow water fringed with weed
and stand absurd, bogged down in mud.

Jane Austen's lovers met again
at Pemberley beside a stream,
and talked politely on the lawn,

so when at Lyme I visit here
where ladies from their belvedere
observed their menfolk hunting deer,

I love these views, old harmony,
each oak and Spanish chestnut tree
designed like Austen's Pemberley.

But out beyond the sports and feasts
lies Manchester, just fifteen miles,
where in those old satanic mills,

in Gaskell's *Mary Barton* world,
hard times for working men produced
the wealth from which Lyme Park was shaped.

And so I'm glad, after the film,
a spinster lady's style and charm
brought TV crowds flocking to see

– in shining cars, not chaise or brougham –
marvels of Darcy's Pemberley.

Privacy

I'm watching Darcy kiss his bride,
and I'm annoyed, for in those days
a public kiss would shock, disgust.

Off in their coach the couple ride
to dream-like Pemberley, its woods
and streams, a life Jane Austen must

have long desired. And so these two
revised their first impressions, tried
to temper passion with good sense.

While Mr Bennet learned to rue
his choice of beauty as his guide,
a lifetime's debt for young romance,

Elizabeth in words and deeds
discovered forms, not fashion's creeds,
where love could thrive in privacy –

mistress at last of Pemberley

Hospital

Appointment at ten; appointment for what?
For men like me the menu's rather skint:
two items on the board, for ten per cent
an early death, while for the lucky ones,
so I was told last time, at least five years
or many more, until the cancer wins.

In waiting rooms like this, sad clocks decide
they'll go on strike, time lingers and
while other patients seem to forge ahead,
I'm left alone, trying to read the news,
the NHS, its chronic lack of beds,
while all I want to hear is my own news.

At last a nurse conducts me to a cell,
hospital grim, where I'm to wait until
the doctor comes. Inspection bed, wash-bowl,
my only faithful friends, I wait alone,
nothing to read, while minutes pass, five, ten.
This is the NHS; if I complain

maybe the hidden gods won't treat me right.
It's twenty now. I need to urinate.
The gleaming wash-bowl tempts. But here at last
my fate arrives; he soon dismisses me.
I've scored OK. I never thought I'd be
so glad he's bored. There's no apology.

Prostate

My doctor's young, but still his words
reflect old-fashioned courtesies.
He shyly says: 'You'll lose desires',

averse to break the social code
which covers up a hidden world:
erections in the marriage bed.

And so at night we lie here chaste,
a little sad for what is lost,
yet all the memories we share

create a stillness richer far
than happy bouts of push and thrust.

Cheshire Walks

For months I've not been strong enough for walks.
The cancer in my bones twitches and nips.

But now my doctor's drugs begin to work.
Past well-known streets I drive to Alison's

– coffee beside the Macclesfield canal –
and then I'll start an old familiar trail.

Today I'll not walk far. The railway line
– disused – leads all the way to Bollington.

The paths that cancer closed beckon and wait.
The Cheshire plain is touched with morning light.

Reservoir

After sickness I'm just a ghost
at odds with woods and morning mist,
at distance from the normal world
of hikers on this Hayfield road.

I've walked this ways so many times,
but never with these double views;
my memories of health distort
the cottages, the mildewed gate

that leads beside a stream towards
a field of tents, white camping cars
I used to drive in days so past
I doubt they ever did exist.

A young man and his girl don't know
the trail that leads to Kinder Low.
We chat, and as they walk away
their human touch transforms my day.

I may be slow, but as I trudge
by Ranger Post and Bowden Bridge
towards the Kinder Reservoir
old memories no longer mar

the famous view to Ashop Head.
I drink my coffee, eat my bread.

The Edge

I walk Hare Hill to Alderley;
after night sweats I feel so free
to sniff afresh new morning air,
to find clear yellow markers where
lush meadows yield to may-time trees.

Once firelit ancients sat and said
that magic nightly filled the woods;
wizards and witches cast their spells;
white horses pranced in secret caves.
For me it's magical to stay
alive, to welcome each new day,
to note once more a bluebell splash,
to sit in shade beneath high beech.

I sweat again in summer heat.
Is it perhaps I'm overweight
or side effects of drugs? Who cares?
Today I'm here. The sun shines on.
Beer waits for me at Wizard Inn.

Lake District

In winter trees I'm resting now,
my forest tucked above the lake.
White-haired hills peer down at me
while overhead geese cross the moon.

Perhaps I'll see the spring again,
when hikers beat the forest trails,
and all the hill-tops turn to green.
The geese fly straight. I don't know where.

Flushes

Hot sweats at dawn disturb my rest.
Two hours before our morning tea,

I meditate, recall my past
those years when happiness for me
meant safe in bed without the threat
of air-raids banging through the night.

I savour silence, lots of time
to try to find a better rhyme.

Manchester United

Three months I've been away. Under the stand,
(where we all sit today), I join the crowd,
in artificial light a mass of red,
scarves, bobble hats, T-shirts with names of stars,

Beckham or Keane, Neville or Giggs.
Queues wait for beer, coffee from plastic cups,
everywhere a buzz, loudspeakers list the teams,
warm welcome for Norwegian visitors,

for little Ben who's eight at his first game.
Afraid I might not last until half-time,
I don't buy drink, just Toblerone
to keep up strength this winter afternoon.

Brick tunnels lead from shadow into light:
the well-known stadium, my third-row seat,
my first-class view across Old Trafford green,
where millionaires parade their skill and brawn.

The fans near me I've known for twenty years;
I don't know where they live, not even names,
united just in worship of United.
I thought they'd ask me where I'd been; instead

nothing: no prostate jokes, no raillery.
At first I'm somewhat miffed. But then I see
that crowds survive by pushing you aside,
by not admitting their mortality.

The game begins. We're totally absorbed.
My illness doesn't matter any more.
When Beckham scores, we stand and clap and cheer.

Old Trafford

I feel somewhat ridiculous.
I hold aloft a photograph
of icon Best the bibulous
– perhaps up there he wants to laugh –

as we observe these formal rites.
Some forty thousand demonstrate
a silent woe which reunites
the men of nineteen sixty-eight

who played with him that famous time
they won the European prize.
Down on the pitch they stand in line,
dark-suited, famous in disguise,

while I recall their younger looks
I watched that day with friends now dead.
I wonder what my grandson thinks
and if he feels too overfed

on memories before his day,
on granddad's tales he's heard before.
He's come to see Ronaldo play:
ten minutes on we watch him score.

In front of us the fans go wild,
raise up their George Best printed sheets
so we can't know what's on the field.
We wait for them to take their seats

– it's never wise to beef – meanwhile
as they repeat their chants and howls
my lad gives me a little smile:
worth more to me than skilful goals.

Sensation

After the heat of motorways
this shallow water feels so cold.
Beside the crowded beach I stand
irresolute, up to my knees,

then charge into the sea, ignore
cold waves sousing my private parts,
find water deep enough at last
to plunge and swim away from shore.

I'm soon acclimatised, and bask
in joy, quickened because I thought
I'd never see this beach from Sète
to Marseillan again. I'm back,

watching French family routines,
long afternoons at play with kites,
the beach boys selling coke and nuts,
while overhead a biplane drags

an advert for a circus spree;
tonight's sensation, so it reads:
mangy lions and fusty clowns
I'd pay good money not to see.

Back at the edge, after my swim,
the shallow water now feels warm.
I rest awhile, perched on my side,
all senses calm and satisfied.

Photographs

Our wonky camera now rests
beneath sad piles of dustbin waste.

We buy a new Olympus, but,
a pagan god, its wiles defeat

our human wit. When we dip south
through France we find the blabbermouth

to whom we paid two hundred pounds
forgot to say its power fades,

and so our friends won't have to see
the jumbo-sized old man that's me,

now overweight from prostate drugs
cavorting on his bare white legs

across the stinging sands at Sète,
waddling the slopes at Lac d'Artouste,

knackered from walks at Arcachon
while others mount the famous dune.

I'm glad because at home I've loads
of snaps, those times I cycled miles

to fall in love with France and wine:
that young man's here. I'm still the same.

Jane Eyre in Derbyshire

Beside – I think – a local stream
Jane Eyre on top of Rochester
communicates such strong desire
it leaps at us across the screen.

I've done without for five good years
– a side-effect of prostate drugs –
so now I feel a slight surprise
that sex so dominates young lives.

My neutral state, this life-long ban,
makes me increasingly aware
our greatest love depends on care
for children, parents, anyone.

I know, in spite of passion, Jane
in Brontë's work would think I'm right.
Next week we'll find the very spot,
saunter beside that stream, and then

we'll find a pub, and rest at ease
with fish and chips and mushy peas.
Maybe you think we're two old wrecks.
Our love goes deep; we don't need sex.

End Game

The day they said 'your cancer's worse'
I walked away through rows of limes
whose autumn leaves recalled old verse
I'd learnt by heart in better times.

Lawrence came first: his Ship of Death;
the falling fruit like drops of dew
scatters across the hardened earth.
And then there's Keats: a rosy hue
on stubble plains, moss'd cottage trees.

As I recalled these well-known lines
music of verse reshaped my news:
a touch of joy in grievous times.

Orhan Pamuk: *My Name is Red*

At Cartaret I watch the coming tide
spreading across amazing yellow sand.
My wife, fitter than me, walks barefoot at
the water's edge, while I perch on a rock,
brooding upon this strange, unsettling book
where men who die recount what happens next.

His skull cleaved through, a murdered man bemoans
his early death, flesh stinking down a well.
He loved his work for sultans, painting vines,
gazelles, horses and hunters, a subtle leaf.
He wants torture, breaking his rival's bones,
and tells us little of the afterlife.

An honest man enjoys his funeral,
so proud to see great crowds of famous men.
I've not read Muslim texts about the soul,
used here in words so beautiful I feel
a possibility, as angels take
the man, at peace, through festivals of light.

I'll soon find out what happens next. Some say
eternity would bore. I don't agree.
I'd watch the changing colours of the sea
with constant joy, thankful to stay alive.
And now my wife approaches with the tide.
Also there's always love, there's always love.